WHITE
TIE
TALES

WHITE TIE TALES

A COLLECTION OF AFTER-DINNER STORIES

John H. Morecroft

BAILEY BROTHERS & SWINFEN LTD
FOLKESTONE

Published in Great Britain by
Bailey Brothers & Swinfen Ltd
1974
Copyright © John H. Morecroft
SBN 561 00236 3

First Reprint 1975

Typesetting by Gyro Repro
Printed in Great Britain by
Whitstable Litho, Straker Brothers Ltd.

To my wife Hilda, without whom . . .

A red carnation for the sinner and a white for the saint. That is the choice everyone has to make when attending the annual dinner of the Saints and Sinners' Club in London. It is a male party and is acknowledged to be one of the most enjoyable functions in the London calendar. As soon as you enter the foyer of the hotel you are met by two charming young ladies, one carrying a basket of red carnations and the other a basket of white. Your conscience must decide which colour you choose.

Prince Philip, when attending the dinner, perhaps not wishing to declare himself in public either a saint or a sinner showed complete impartiality by wearing his own pink carnation.

It is quite permitted for one's conscience to change from year to year like that of Lord Birkett, famous both as a barrister and a Law Lord. In 1954 he selected a red carnation and told me simply: "I am a sinner". The following year he wore both and in 1961, when he had changed to white, he told me: "I am growing older and wiser". Everyone who is anyone in their own particular professions, the law, music, sport or the stage, attends these dinners. Viscount Amory explained with a smile, when choosing the badge of the sinner: "It is for my political crimes". Arthur Askey wore one of the same colour in 1964 but asked for a mauve one and then when he changed to white the next year declared: "I have turned over a new life". Freddie Mills, the boxer, chose red and said to me: "I am not going to be a sinner", while Aneurin Bevan, the forthright politician with the voice of a charmer said, as he selected a red carnation: "If I chose a white one they would not believe me".

Mr. Justice Edmund Davies, explaining his choice of red, said: "It is just modesty".

It would be expected that a journalist who had spent nearly thirty years reporting at the world's most famous criminal court, the Old Bailey, would write about traitors, spies, murders, rape or violence when he retired.

"But I have seen enough tears and tragedy in the courts and would now like to do something to cheer people up", says the author, John H. Morecroft.

At the end of the Second World War he joined the reporting staff of the Press Association and was soon assigned to the Old Bailey. He claims that until he retired in 1972 he had seen more murderers than anyone else in the country. Possibly as a form of mental relaxation he attended banquets about twice a week to report the speeches. After watching judges and barristers all day, dressed in their wigs, robes and gowns, he would himself dress in dinner jacket or white tie and tails at night and would go and dine with the famous at Guildhall, the Mansion House or Livery Halls in the City of London or at the Savoy, Grosvenor House, the Dorchester or at Claridges in the West End. Whenever he heard an anecdote or joke from the thousands of speeches he has had to listen to he would record it in his note-book. The note-books are stored away in hundreds with the jokes sandwiched between pages of evidence of some of the country's most notorious criminal trials.

The cartoons by Giles are reproduced from the menu of the "Saints and Sinners" Club of London by the kind permission of the founder and Hon. Secretary, Mr. Percy Hoskins.

It should be noted that the titles, offices and positions of the speakers were those they held at the time of the function.

"My Lords, Ladies & Gentlemen . . ."

A sudden silence falls on the babble of the voices of the diners as the scarlet-coated toast-master raps the table with his gavel. Then up gets a speaker and within a few moments his audience will know whether they are going to hear a good speech or a boring one.

What makes a good speaker? And what makes a good speech? Some men are born to it and take it in their stride while others have to try to acquire the technique and sweat blood and tears before and while on their feet. Some are blessed with a voice that charms, like Lord Birkett, Aneurin Bevan and the former Old Bailey Judge, John Maude, Q.C. Whenever they spoke and whatever they said you listened to them with sheer pleasure. Others have mannerisms or facial expressions that capture and hold your attention; while others have a smooth, lucid flow, like Lord Mancroft and the Recorder of London (Sir Carl Aarvold) and you cannot but listen to them with rapt attention.

Others are no good at making speeches and go out of their way to tell their audience so from the very start. The professional speaker knows all the tricks of the trade and employs them to the full, but a few words to the amateur who has to make a speech once in a while — and dreads it — might not come amiss.

Don't rush through a speech. Speak slowly and distinctly and enunciate clearly. If you drop your words at the end of a sentence the interest of the diners will drop too. Rehearse it with the aid of a tape recorder. Even if you have not the expression and delivery of a Churchill you can, at least, find something interesting to say that will hold the attention of your audience. Whatever you say don't be a bore. If speaking at the normal dinner remember your audience is anxious to be amused, not bored with a tedious speech. You will find they will react on the slightest provocation to humour. Keep the heavy stuff for the annual meeting or the trade journal. Make them laugh and the applause at the end will indicate how it was appreciated.

Some years ago I attended a dinner in Park Lane, London and the first speaker was the chairman. Heavily-built, ageing and non-descript, he started to read his speech. The members of the professional organisation, accompanied by their wives, settled down, after a good dinner and wine ad lib, to listen attentively. Facts and figures poured out from the chairman, comparing one year's products with another and pointing out what should be done in the future and what should have been done in the past. He had a dreary voice and it was all said in a quiet monotone.

The diners began to get restive and remarks were passed between the individual tables. The toast-master noticed this and appreciating the developing situation tried to stop it by waving his arms from where he stood behind the chairman.

The speaker, not noticing this, plodded on reading his prepared speech. His eyes were only for the typescript and not once did he glance up. He then had silence for a few minutes until about a dozen diners at one of the tables could stand it no longer. They began "ringing the glasses". If you moisten your finger and rub it lightly round a wine glass rim it will emit a clear penetrating bell-like tone. Other tables took it up and soon from one end of the banqueting hall to the other came the mellifluous notes. Then the toast-master took an unheard of action. He stopped the chairman in the middle of his address. Rapping the table with his gavel he commanded silence and in a voice seldom heard from toast-masters told the diners: "Your chairman is addressing you. Please have the courtesy to pay him the respect due to him". The shame-faced diners fell silent. The chairman looked up from his notes, glanced around, and then continued his dreary speech right to the end.

The lesson from that is never bore your audience — especially if they are just waiting for the speeches to finish in order to start dancing.

You have to speak according to your audience. What may be understood and acceptable to your own circle or profession may have disastrous results on another. I well remember a dinner-dance in the West End. The principal speaker was a surgeon from the provinces. He began in an orthodox way speaking about nothing in particular and then started to describe one of his operations. The effect on his audience was dramatic, and so far as the ladies were concerned, literally overwhelming. They began fainting all over the place. Waiters began rushing about with carafes of cold water and the men did what they could by waving their table napkins. I saw about twenty ladies in a dead faint carried out and about a dozen "walking cases" were helped out. Out in the foyer the twenty lay unconscious on the floor in a long row. The waiters could not take them into the Powder Room because they were male waiters. The speaker stopped in surprise at what he saw before him and then hurried out into the foyer and began attending the ladies and doing what he could to repair the damage caused by his unwitting and thoughtless remarks.

Always consider your audience — and their physical comforts. Some years ago an experiment was tried at the Mansion House, the official residence of the Lord Mayor of London, with unexpected results.

Banquets are held there every week throughout the year, and in the summer time the temperature sometimes gets a bit warm for the men in their white ties, starched shirts and tails and the ladies in their evening dresses. Accordingly, to cool the atmosphere, large blocks of ice are put on the long tables placed at right angles to the top table. The sight of the ice a few feet away from you may have a good psychological effect and help you to feel cool. One year the banqueting manager decided to have small table fountains on the tables instead of ice. With the light from the candles playing on the cascading water the result was most effective. But then came the speeches. There were so many interruptions by the men paying a quick visit outside that the fountains were never used again. The psychological effect of the sight of running water was one that had not been envisaged.

The important point to remember is to keep your speech bright and crisp. In the following pages can be found anecdotes that can be incorporated into speeches for all occasions. Use them. They have been said at public dinners by people in the highest circles in the land, by famous churchmen and politicians and by people well-known in industry and the professions. Time and time again I have heard the same basic jokes trotted out by various people in varied forms and they always go down well.

GENERAL...
cabbages
and
kings

Viscount Amory, at Retail Distributors Association dinner, Savoy Hotel, 1967:

A tom cat was keeping residents awake and they appealed to the owner to have it destroyed. The owner had a surgical operation performed on the cat and it was hoped the neighbours would be able to sleep in peace. But the noise at night was no better. The neighbours joined forces one night with the object of catching the cat and killing it. They found it caterwauling on a large lawn surrounded by a group of young toms. The moral is if you can't be a practitioner at least you can be a consultant.

Mr. Geoffrey D. Blake, President of Chartered Auctioneers and Estate Agents Institute, at their dinner, Dorchester Hotel, June 28, 1956:

Everyone who has lived within four walls is an expert on housing. Most of them suffer from one of the common human frailties — over estimation of their own goods. Quite frequently we find ourselves explaining to our clients that geese are not swans but are white elephants.

Sir Cecil Wakely, past president of Royal College of Surgeons at dinner of Society of Yorkshiremen in London, Dorchester Hotel, November 15, 1956:

A young fellow had a car accident and was taken to hospital unconscious. When he regained consciousness he asked the nurse: "Have I come here to die?" She replied, "You came here yesterdie".

Duke of Edinburgh at dinner of French Chamber of Commerce in Great Britain, 1963:

French with an English accent has a certain limited use. I think it was Lloyd George who said that the only person who could understand his French was his friend the Foreign Secretary, Sir Edward Grey.

Statesmen are naturally in special danger and, as you know, Winston Churchill had his own brand of French. His own wit produced a classic story. At the end of the war he appeared in France in the uniform of an Elder Brethren of Trinity House. Clemenceau was surprised and asked him what the uniform was. "Je suis la frère de la Trinitie", said Churchill. It was too much for Clemenceau, who said: "Mon Dieu, quelle influence".

Stories of misunderstanding are legion and are known as fractured French. Pas de deux as father of twins, and Mal de mere as Mother-in-law. There are a number of mistranslations of that famous motto "Honi Soit Qui Mal Y Pense". The latest I have heard is "I honestly believe I am going to be sick".

Naturally the last war produced a splendid crop of mistranslations. A pilot presented himself at a farmhouse in France and said: "J'ai crashe dans les rognons", which, I understand, when translated, means "I've spit in the kidneys".

All our menus are in French. In New Zealand we entertained a famous girl swimmer on board to dinner. Afterwards she was asked by friends what she had had and she replied: "I don't know. It was all in French".

Lord Kilmuir, at dinner of Guild of Cordwainers, at House of Commons, November 26, 1954:

For the first time in a long experience the chairman has not turned to me and said: "Shall we let them enjoy themselves a little longer or will you begin your speech?"

Mr. Reginald Maudling, at dinner of Institute of Cost & Works Accountants, 1965:

Four men, in a railway carriage, all sitting in opposite corners and saying nothing. After an hour one stood up and said: "This is going to be a very dull journey if we don't talk," and said by way of introduction: "I am a brigadier and have three sons, all accountants". The second said: "I am a brigadier and have three sons all barristers". The third said: "I am a brigadier and have three sons all solicitors". The fourth sat silently in his corner until he was asked: "How about you?" and he answered: "I am a sergeant-major, married and I have three sons all brigadiers".

Mr. R.A. Butler, former Minister of Education, National Association Corn and Agriculture Merchants, Dorchester Hotel, February 14, 1949:

A Scotsman gave his girl friend a present of a lipstick — so that he would get half of it back.

Lord Lucas of Chilworth, Private Secretary, Minister of Transport, National Association of Furniture Warehousemen, Jubilee dinner, Park Lane Hotel, May 3, 1950:

I have lived long enough to know there is no fun in respectability.

Mr. R.A. Butler, Anglo-Jewish Association dinner, Dorchester Hotel, June 1, 1951:

An after dinner speech should be like a lady's dress — long enough to cover the subject and short enough to be interesting.

Sir Paul Batchell at Calcutta dinner, Connaught Rooms, May 24, 1951:

The Brahmin bulls can still be found wandering up and down the steps of a famous bank in Calcutta and are said to be the biggest depositors.

Lord Justice Morris, Society of Yorkshiremen in London, Dorchester Hotel, November 12, 1953:

What Yorkshire and Lancashire think today England will do its best to pronounce tomorrow.

Sir Miles Thomas, Chairman of B.O.A.C. at dinner of Association of Supervising Electrical Engineers, Connaught Rooms, April 2, 1954:

A man took Harpic in mistake for Enos and went clean round the bend.

14

Mr. W. Charles Norton, President of the Law Society, at Building Societies Institute dinner, Hyde Park Hotel, March 8, 1956:

When I was a very young man my father took me to see the Lord Chief Justice of the day, who was renowned for his after-dinner speeches. I took the opportunity of asking him whether he would tell me the principles he applied when making his speeches. He said: "First, you should refer to the importance of the occasion. Of course, any occasion on which I am called upon to speak is an important occasion. Secondly, you should refer to the weakness of the vessel by which the toast is proposed. Of course you need not stress that because your audience will soon find that out for itself. Thirdly, if there is time, and only if there is time, should you make some reference to the subject of the toast".

Frank Shires, President of Food Manufacturers Federation at dinner of Institute of Meat, Innholder's Hall, London E.C., April 28, 1952:

A new employee of a dairy dashed into a lavatory and was about to hurry out afterwards when the manager drew his attention to a notice: "Wash your hands before Working". The youth replied: "Oh, that's alright. I am only going to lunch."

Lord Lloyd of Dolobran at East Africa Club dinner, Connaught Rooms, June 20, 1956:

Lord Birkenhead attended a meeting to give a talk. When asked for his address by the chairman, he stood up, said "48 Grosvenor Square", and went home.

Lord Justice of Appeal, Sir Norman Birkett, at Chartered Auctioneers and Estate Agents Institute dinner, Dorchester Hotel, June 28, 1956:

I was speaking to a visitor from California and mentioned our dull summer. He replied: "In California we have 365 days of sunshine every year — and that is a conservative estimate".

I learned with great interest of the man who took his dog to the cinema and who sat it in the seat beside him. The dog would yelp with pleasure at intervals when watching the film. Told that it was an extraordinary thing that the dog should appreciate the film, the man replied: "Yes it is, because he simply hated the book".

A lady travelling in a train saw a man tearing a newspaper into tiny pieces and, at intervals, throwing them out of the window. She asked him why, and he said they were to keep the elephants away. When she said: "But there are no elephants", he answered: "Yes, it is wonderfully effective".

Bernard Shaw went to a dinner and on his return home was asked if he had enjoyed himself. He answered: "I enjoyed myself because there was nothing else there to enjoy".

Lord Goddard, Lord Chief Justice of England, at State banquet by Lord Mayor of London to Her Majesty's Judges, Mansion House, July 11, 1956:

You have to be very careful what you say in public, because if you say anything ambiguous and the papers publish it the wrong interpretation is always given to it. For instance, a kind old lady employed a chauffeur who was taken to hospital with a sudden appendix. She visited him and was asked by the ward sister: "Are you his wife?". "No", she replied, "I am his mistress".

Lord Chief Justice of England, Lord Goddard, at State banquet by Lord Mayor of London to Her Majesty's judges, Mansion House, July 1, 1956:

There was an old tipster known to all the racing fraternity as Old George. He used to go round to all the race meetings throughout the country. His tips got worse and worse and one day, by Hurst Park, his body was recovered from the river. It was taken to the mortuary to await identification. His closest friend arrived and he was asked to identify him. He was shown three bodies but not that of Old George. The friend suddenly burst out laughing and when asked by the Coroner's officer for the reason, replied: "Just like Old George, right up to the end, never in the first three".

Dr. Charles Hill, Post-Master General, London Chamber of Commerce dinner, Grosvenor House, September 4, 1956:

". . . our relations over the years with the Chamber have been just right. This reminds me of the Colonel of the regiment who presented a barrel of beer to the Officers' Mess. It was duly sampled and passed on to the Sergeants' Mess. The following day the Adjutant asked the sergeant-major how they had liked the beer. "It was just right", he replied. "Just right? What do you mean?" asked the Adjutant. "Well, sir", replied the sergeant-major, "If it had been any better we would not have got it. And if it had been any worse we would not have been able to drink it".

GENERAL

Lord Justice Birkett, at dinner of Society of Yorkshiremen in London, Dorchester Hotel, November 15, 1956:

The chairman of a great university wanted some well-known speaker for his annual dinner. He sent a letter to a friend saying the man he wanted would have to be a wit. The friend replied saying he could not get the man who had been suggested but enclosed the suggestion that instead of getting a wit he should have two half wits.

During a County Court hearing, the defendant cried out: "As God is my judge I do not owe the money". The Judge retorted: "He isn't. I am. You do. Pay up."

Lord Kilmuir, Lord Chancellor, at dinner of Lloyd Memorial Home (Printing Trade), Connaught Rooms, December 3, 1959:

A countryman of mine sent his chauffeur to wait for his wife in the car. A friend of the chauffeur arrived and asked him who he was waiting for. The chauffeur replied: "I'm waiting for Lord John's fat old besom". The wife overheard and told her husband. She told him to take the chauffeur to task. Asked later if he had done so, the husband replied: "I told him that it is not for the likes of him to tell you what you are".

Sir Miles Thomas, British Chemical Plant Manufacturers Association dinner, Grosvenor House, October 9, 1958:

Normally when one gets up to respond to the toast of guests one usually has not a lot of literature and one feels like a dog that has gone down a street full of lamp posts but short of material and finds he has hardly a leg to stand on.

18

Lord Mancroft, Minister without Portfolio, at dinner of Auctioneers and Estate Agents, Dorchester Hotel, October 31, 1957:

A nightwatchman recently described himself in court as a Noctitian, and a cat's meat man as a Feline Alimentary Distributor. Last year the sanitary engineers suggested they should be known as Public Health Officers. We should be lucky they did not want to call themselves Privy Counsellors".

Lord Mancroft, Parliamentary Secretary, Ministry of Defence, Retail Distributors Association dinner, Savoy, May 1, 1957:

When I was at the Home Office I was sent to the afforestation area on the border of Wales, as I was to look after Welsh affairs. The director of the area complained bitterly about the litter left by tourists. I asked him: "Are you not in some way to blame for not having enough litter baskets?" He assured me there were quite enough litter baskets for the purpose. The next day I went into the area and on turning a corner I saw an immense litter basket with the words "Put Your Litter Here", in Welsh, I suppose to keep the Welsh nationalists happy, and the request in English so that it could be understood. I went round another corner and found a bigger litter basket and then round a third corner and found a still bigger basket. I told the verderer in charge: "This is first class and it is just what I want to see". The verderer looked at me and said: "First class, yes, and just what you wanted to see. Damn me, so they should be. We were up all the bloody night making them".

Lord Simmonds, Lord Chancellor, at Lord Mayor of London's dinner to Her Majesty's Judges, Mansion House, July 8, 1954:

The first time I met you, Lord Mayor, was at the House of Lords when you came to visit me in accordance with ancient tradition and we had a stoup of wine. I have visited you at the Mansion House many times since then and on every one you were about to drink, or were drinking or had just been drinking. If I was asked what the Lord Mayor of London does I really would not know what he does except drink.

Duke of Bedford, Association of British Travel Agents, Dorchester Hotel, November 18, 1957:

I always try to please the customers who visit me at my house, Woburn Abbey, and I asked a visitor: "Have you enjoyed going over the place?" The woman walked past the million and a half pounds worth of art treasures looking down at the serviceable but useful linoleum on the floor, and said: "This is what I like best. I would like to get some for my kitchen". That is part of the fun of being in the stately home business.

Sir John Dalton, President of British Electric Power Convention, dinner of Electrical Power Engineers Association, Connaught Rooms, November 25, 1955:

An American gave a swimming bath to a lunatic asylum and called one day to see how it was received. He was welcomed rather quietly by the doctors and nurses. He stopped an attendant in the grounds and asked how the patients liked the bath. "They love it", he said, "They push each other over the side all day long and there is always a queue waiting to go down the chute. God knows what it is going to be like when we put the water in".

Dr. J.A. Scott, Queen's Hon. Physician & Chairman of Royal Society of Health, dinner of Institute of Meat, Innholder's Hall, E.C., May 19, 1958:

Definition of an adult: One who has stopped growing, except in the middle.

Definition of a baby: An alimentary canal that makes a lot of noise at one end and has no sense of responsibility at the other.

Advertisement in an American draper's shop: Divinity may shape your ends. But if it doesn't we have the best girdles in town.

Advertisement in American newspaper: Young lady seeks job as secretary, willing to struggle if given the chance.

Beautiful evening gown, worn only once. Exchange for baby carriage.

The following are absolutely true letters received by Ministry of Pensions:

"Please find out if my husband is dead as the man I am living with won't do anything until I am certain".

And from another lady:

"I want the money as soon as possible. I have been in bed with the doctor for a week and he doesn't seem to be doing me any good."

Lord Milligan, at dinner of The Highland Society of London, Grosvenor House, July 15, 1964:

A bad golf player kept losing balls and his caddie said to him: "Don't you think it would be better and cheaper if you played with some old balls?" The player replied: "I have never had a ball long enough to be old."

Minister of Health, at Faculty of Dental Surgery of Royal College of Surgeons dinner, July 18, 1958:

I only hope the entrants to your profession are not handicapped in the way a young student was who took his finals in his honours degree in economics. He was a little surprised to find the examination papers were exactly the same as the previous year when he took his intermediate. He drew the attention of the examiner to this strange fact, who told him: "You are quite wrong about this. It is quite true the questions are the same but remember this is economics and the answers this year are quite different."

Lord Irwan, Chief Steward of Jockey Club, dinner of Victoria Club, Grosvenor House, March 10, 1959:

When asked to make a speech I felt like the young man who had to make his first speech. He was in a bit of a twitch and consulted a writer friend. The friend told him there was nothing to worry about and that all attending dinners were exactly alike and were interested in only four subjects — religion, aristocracy, sex and mystery. The youth thought about this, acted on it and made his first speech as arranged. It was: "Good God", said the duchess, "I am pregnant. Who did it?"

Mr. T.R. Priest, president, Radio and Television Retailers Association, Park Lane Hotel, October 26, 1954:

There is a controversy raging amongst educationalists regarding intelligence. Some say that in junior schools intelligence is found to be more forward in girls than in boys, while in secondary schools it is more pronounced in boys than in girls. But in co-ed schools it is found to be neck and neck.

Mr. Roy Thomson, newspaper proprietor, at dinner of Institute of Public Relations, 1962:

One of my Canadian papers carried a story about a detective who had arrested a man and by a typographical error said the arrest was made by Defective Williams. The officer protested and the editor agreed to correct it. The next day the paper had a corrected paragraph: "The arrest was made by Detective Williams of the local police farce".

Earl of Courtown, President of Institute of Office Management, at their dinner at the Kensington Palace Hotel, October 4, 1960:

An attempt was made to make use of an electronic machine to translate English into Russian. The phrase "Out of sight, out of mind" was fed into the machine. The answer came out in Russian and this was fed back into the machine to be translated into English. The answer came out: "Invisible idiot".

Ernest Marples, Post Master General, Telecommunications Engineering and Manufacturing Association dinner, May Fair Hotel, November 12, 1958:

When we carried out a survey of pensioners we found we got answers we did not expect. One man of 75 said he would like to die in a train crash; a man of 88 said he would like to die in a plane crash; and a man of 99 said he would like to die being chased by a jealous husband.

In a Scottish post office blotting paper used to disappear. When people complained the following notice was displayed: "Blotting paper will not be provided until people stop taking it away".

Dr. Charles Hill, Chancellor of the Duchy of Lancaster, at Allied Brewery Trades Association dinner, Grosvenor House, March 21, 1960:

I recall the patient who complained at the hospital that the bed pan had not been changed since the Battle of Waterloo, only to be reminded by the ward sister: "Nor has the shape of the human bottom".

The perfect host makes his guests feel at home — when he wishes they were.

I feel like the small boy in a general knowledge examination, when asked to name two ancient sports, promptly replied: "Anthony and Cleopatra".

Two maiden ladies lived together with their cat Tibby. One received an offer of marriage which was promptly accepted and she was married. The fortunate sister promised to write to the other telling her what married life was like. Three days after the marriage the spinster received a telegram from her sister: "Let Tibby out tonight."

Dr. Charles Hill, Minister of Housing and Local Government, and Minister for Welsh Affairs, at National Federation of Building Trades Employers, Grosvenor House, February 6, 1962:

Two conferences were held at Brighton and were held in the same building. One was a newspaper proprietors federation and the other was a federation of fish and chip fryers. It was not long before they each realised that the business of one was wrapped up in the business of the other.

Lord Mancroft, Incorporated Sales Managers' Association dinner, Claridge's, February 10, 1960:

In an attempt to raise the standard of relations between the juvenile population of West Ham and the police, a headmaster asked his boys to write an essay about the police. Willy, aged 11, wrote his essay in one sentence: "The police is baskets." This shocked the headmaster, who wrote to the local police super-intendent. The superintendent wrote to Willy inviting him along to the station. Willy went along, and the superintendent, to get him interested and to gain his friendship, showed him over the station and cells and allowed him to blow his whistle and play with the handcuffs. Little Willy was then taken home in a police car with the gong sounding. The next day he had to write another essay on the same subject. The essay he wrote consisted again of only one sentence, but it was a bit longer. It was: "The police is crafty baskets".

Sir Robert Shone, Director General of National Economic Development Council, at dinner of Joint Iron Council, Dorchester Hotel, November 7, 1962:

A reporter went to interview a couple celebrating their golden wedding and asked them how they had enjoyed their lives. The old man replied: "We have been happily wed all these years because in the home I make all the big decisions and my wife makes all the small ones". Asked what the small decisions were, he answered: "What we do generally; where we go for our holidays, what we eat, who our friends are, who to invite to the house, when to go to bed and when to get up, and things like that". Asked the reporter: "What are the big decisions you make?" The husband answered: "Such things as who will be the next president of the United States, the question of Europe's economy, the settling of the Middle East problems, and all matters concerning disarmament".

Lord Mayor of London, Sir Denis Truscott, at Canada Club dinner, Savoy, July 2, 1958:

There were eleven brothers. The first was an accountant and the second was no good at figures either; the third was a solicitor and the fourth was a rogue also; the fifth was a financier and the sixth was in a cell next to him; the seventh won the O.B.E. and the eighth had not seen any fighting either; the ninth was a Canadian and the tenth had a funny accent too; while the eleventh was a batchelor just like his father.

Schoolboy howler: People in this country are allowed only one wife — and that is called monotony.

Little girl said to another: My father must be very fond of animals because I heard him tell my mother: "I put my shirt on a bleeding horse that was scratched".

Mr. Robin Turton, M.P., at dinner of Incorporated Society of Auctioneers and Landed Property Agents, November 10, 1960:

A temperance speaker came to my constituency and tried to convert my constituents to temperance. He took two glasses, filled one with clean water and the other with whiskey. From his pocket he took a little tin box and from the box a wriggling worm. He dropped the worm into the water and the worm seemed quite happy. Then he took it out and dropped it in the glass with the whiskey. Immediately the worm stretched out and died. The lecturer asked the audience, "Now, what is the lesson of that?" One old fellow rose, scratched his head and replied: "If thou'st suffering from worms tha must drink tha whiskey neat".

Lord Statham, dinner of National Federation of Building Trades Employers, Grosvenor House, February 6, 1962:

A gastronome attended a banquet in London and heard from other gastronomical colleagues talk of a fabulous dish called Poy. It could be obtained, he was told, in only one place in the world. Full of curiosity, he inquired where it was. None of his colleagues had had it but all had heard of it. One knew where the village was where it could be obtained. "You go up to Katmandu, up and over the pass, turn right in the middle of the highest village and you will find it at the second monastery on the left." The gourmet organised an expedition. He flew to Katmandu, hired guides and carriers and set off. After months of climbing up mountains and down valleys and up mountains again he came to the monastery. He rang the great bell and a monk answered. "I have come all the way from London to sample your world-famed dish known as Poy", he said. "That is curious", replied the monk. "The cook himself comes from London. I did not know his dish, which he calls Poy, had become world famous. Which of the two will you sample, Shepherd's Poy or Steak and Kidney Poy?"

Sir Thomas Macdonald, High Commissioner for New Zealand, at New Zealand Society dinner, Savoy, February 5, 1964:

A travelling circus visited a small town in Australia and the elephant strayed. A widow, looking out of her window into her garden, saw the elephant among her vegetables and telephoned the circus. "Your elephant is pulling out my carrots with its tail", she complained. The ring-master replied: "We will collect it at once but let me assure you it is not pulling out your carrots with its tail". "Well, I can see it from here with my two eyes", replied the woman. "You may be right", said the man, "but what is it doing with those carrots?"

GENERAL

Sir Thomas Lund, Secretary of the Law Society, at Building Societies Institute dinner, Quaglino's, June 10, 1964:

My best work is done sitting down — and that is where I shine.

A director of a company met a friend unexpectedly in a remote country hotel and explained: "I have come here for a little peace and quiet". The friend answered: "If you'll introduce me to the little piece I'll keep quiet about it."

A one-time wealthy man was asked in a bankruptcy court to what he attributed his insolvency and he replied that he thought it was due to his large collection of old masters in his house and exactly the reverse in his London flat.

Sir Leary Constantine, High Commissioner, West Indies, dinner of Canada Club, Savoy, November 27, 1963:

When playing in a famous match at the Oval I was just walking down the steps of the pavilion going in to bat when I heard someone say I was wanted on the telephone. As I got near to the phone, I heard him say: "He is just going in to bat, will you hold on?"

Mr. Justice Arthian Davies, dinner of Chartered Auctioneers and Estate Agents Institute, Grosvenor House, November 5, 1964:

During the severe winter of two years ago a delegate at a South Wales conference spoke for an hour. When he sat down in complete silence, he turned and asked a neighbour: "What was that like Dy?" Dy replied: "You have shortened the bloody winter for us anyway".

The Duke of Devonshire, Minister of State for Commonwealth Relations, at dinner of Traders Road Transport Association, Grosvenor House, April 29, 1963:

I had a disappointing experience of speech-making not long ago. I was about to make a speech, the thought of which made me extremely nervous. As the vital moment drew near I turned to my neighbour and remarked: "I do hate making speeches". "Do you?", he replied, adding: "I don't mind a bit, but what bores me is listening to them".

Sir Thomas Lund, secretary of Law Society, at Building Societies Institute, Quaglino's, June 10, 1964:

A lad of 13 had to explain how cricket is played and this was his answer: "You have two sides, one out in the field and one in. Each man on the side that's in goes out and when he's out he comes in and the next man goes in until he's out. When they are all out the side that's been out in the field comes in and the side that's been in goes out and tries to get those coming in out. Then when both sides have been in and out, including not-outs, that's the end of the game".

Mr. Boyd Carpenter, Minister of Transport and Civil Aviation, dinner of Institute of Export, Connaught Rooms, December 14, 1955:

A schoolboy was told to write an essay on King Alfred and the teacher warned him not to give the incident of the cakes. The boy accordingly wrote: "King Alfred went round the countryside and at last came to a cottage. He knocked on the door and the lady said her husband was out. She invited him in and I am not allowed to say what happened after that".

Lord Mayor of London, Sir James Miller, dinner of Chartered Institute of Secretaries, Guildhall, December 8, 1964:

One of the best examples of compromise I know took place in a little Scottish borough. The Provost, visiting the city chambers, passed the Town Clerk's room, and looking through the window saw the typist sitting on his knee. For a little Scottish borough that was not good enough, and the Provost called a meeting of the Town Council to decide what to do. A suggestion was made that they should get rid of the Town Clerk. But he was a good Town Clerk and they are difficult to come by. Then the suggestion was made they should sack the typist. But she was a good typist and they are even more difficult to find and keep than a good Town Clerk. It seemed they were in a real predicament until a little man in the corner offered the suggestion which was acted upon — and that was that they should buy a blind for the window.

Sir Harold Howitt, vice-president, dinner of Chartered Accountants Students Society of London, Grosvenor House, December 12, 1955:

A speaker at a dinner went on and on and on. A diner told the chairman: "Hit him on the head with your mallet". The chairman struck out but by a mistake hit the guest of honour. The guest of honour started to slowly disappear under the table semi-conscious and was then heard to mutter: "Hit me again, I can still hear him".

Mr. A.H. Keates, past president Institute of Hospital Management, Connaught Rooms, May 16, 1961:

The perfect civil servant is the man who has a valid objection to any possible solution.

Lord Mayor of London, Sir Frederick Hoare, at dinner of First International Conference of Oral Surgery, Guildhall, July 3, 1962:

A few weeks ago one of our famous hostesses gave a big dinner to a most distinguished gathering. She had invited the Aga Khan's father but because of protocol did not know where he should be seated. She wrote to Debrett and they answered: "The Aga Khan is considered by his millions of followers throughout the world to be directly descended from God. An English duke takes precedence".

Mr. Justice Edmund Davies, at Saints and Sinners Club dinner, Dorchester, April 9, 1962:

Last night I was playing bridge. I am not very good at the game but I am one of those tiresome people who are always wanting to learn. As my partner was Sir Anthony Hawke, the Recorder of London, who is a player of international stature, I took advantage of a lull in the game and asked him: "Tell me how you would have played that last hand of mine?" To my surprise he hissed at me: "If I had to play that last hand as you played it I would have played it under an assumed name."

The Earl of Perth, at The Highland Society of London dinner, Grosvenor House, July 15, 1964:

It became obvious to neighbours of a new tenant of a grouse moor that he was not an experienced shot. But they were pleased when he told them: "I do not want to sell any of the game I shoot but propose to send it to the local hospital". The neighbours thought it was very generous of him. They went to his first shoot and two guns, four beaters and one dog went to the hospital.

31

Sir Edward Reid, president of Overseas Banker's Club dinner, Guildhall, February 1, 1965:

A man had two watches. One gained a second every hour and the other would not go at all. The question was put to a computer as to which watch he should keep. The computer replied:"Keep the watch that does not go". Asked why, it replied: "The watch that does not go will show the exact time once in every twelve hours, but the other watch will only give the right time once every five years".

Mr. H.J.B. Harding, at dinner of Old Centralians (City & Guilds Engineering Association) Grocer's Livery Hall, November 29, 1954:

Mr. Churchill visited Harwell and on being introduced to a scientist, asked him what his work was. "I make heavy water into uranium", answered the scientist. Churchill moved on and asked another scientist in another department what he did. "I make light water to make uranium". Churchill remarked: "I want to make ordinary water but I can't find the urinium".

Lord McCorquodale of Newton, President of British Employers Federation, at dinner of National Joint Industry Council for Rubber Industry, Guildhall, September 26, 1961:

When I was a member for York the local bishop, who liked to attend banquets, would glance at the menu before saying grace. If he approved the menu he would intone: "Oh, bountiful Creator . . ." When the fare was only so-so, he would start: "Oh merciful Lord . . .". On one occasion, showing his lack of approval of the food, he began: "Oh Lord for this the least of all Thy mercies . . .".

Mr. J.R. Malcolmson, president of the Institute of British Launderers, at dinner of the London Section, Savoy, January 6, 1956:

A spinster had her somewhat belated engagement announced in a local newspaper by mistake. When confronted with it, she blushed and said: "Modesty compels me to deny it but thank Heaven for the rumour".

An Irishman, telling a friend of the narrow escape he had had during the war, said: "The bullet entered my left breast and came out at the back". The friend said: "If that had happened the bullet would have gone through your heart and killed you." The Irishman answered: "Begom, my heart was in my mouth at the time".

Two fathers were discussing their sons and their educational abilities. Asked one: "What is your boy going to be when he leaves college?" and the other answered: "It looks as if he is going to be an old man".

Charles Chaplin, dinner of Dickens Fellowship, Cafe Royal, February 7, 1955:

About 25 years ago I was at a dinner sitting next to Sir Winston Churchill. I was terrified that during my speech I might not say the right thing. Then I rose in my seat with every good will in the world and every intention of wanting to remind him and all present of his past glories. I began: "My lords, ladies and gentlemen, as the late Chancellor of the Exchequer has just said . . ." Amidst the confusion that followed I heard Sir Winston saying: "I like that, I like that". Then, in the confusion, I went on: "It is not so peculiar to say ex-Chancellor of the Exchequer but I think the ghost has done extremely well since".

Lord Pearce, Treasurer of Lincoln's Inn, at dinner of Faculty of Anaesthetists, 1966:

A young cadet officer found he was marching his men towards a precipice and became so nervous that he became tongue-tied and could not shout the order to halt or about-turn. At last his sergeant-major shouted to him: "For God's sake say something, even if it is only goodbye".

Lord Netherthorpe, at Livery dinner of Worshipful Company of Farmers, Mansion House, January 22, 1961:

The viewpoint is always a peculiar thing. I remember at a Russian ambassadorial party in Washington when the vodka flowed freely, the British ambassador was challenged by the Russian ambassador to a race. He won.

The next day the Times reported that a race took place between the British and Russian ambassadors in Washington and that the British ambassador won. Curiously enough Pravda also reported it, quite truthfully: "A race took place at Washington. The Russian ambassador was second but the British ambassador was last but one".

Mr. Ernest Marples, Minister of Transport, Chamber of Shipping dinner, Grosvenor House, October 5, 1961:

Three ship owners had lunch costing £20. Afterwards, one said: "Let me pay. I pay supertax at 19/6 in the pound and this bill will only cost me 10/-." The second said: "No, let me pay. I pay excess profits tax and it will cost me nothing". The third said: "I am the one who will pay. I am on cost-plus and I will make a profit from it".

Lord Mancroft, former Minister-without-Portfolio, International Design Congress dinner, Clothworkers Hall, October 4, 1961:

Shortly after war started I was told to lecture a squad of recruits on the Barr and Stroud range finder, mark 2. Well, I knew all about it because just previously I had been told what it was and had been allowed to have one glance through it. The lecture went off very well and I was surprised how much I could tell them. Then near the end a little, quiet-looking recruit began to ask one of those sorts of questions which, unless stopped at once would end in an embarrassing situation so far as I was concerned. I had to stop the question at all costs and fell back on heavy sarcasm. I demanded: "How long have you been in the Army?" He replied: "Three days with the army, sir, and 16 years with Barr & Stroud."

Sir Roger Makins, chairman of the Atomic Energy Authority, at Institute of Fuel dinner, Grosvenor House, October 10, 1961:

My scientific education is at the stage of the schoolboy, of whom it was written: The improvement in the legibility of his hand-writing is beginning to reveal great deficiencies in his spelling".

Lord Kilmuir, former Lord Chancellor, at Independence Day dinner of the American Society in London, July 4, 1961:

A schoolboy asked his teacher if he could be punished for something he had not done. "Of course not, Tommy, that would be quite wrong", replied the teacher. And then Tommy told him, "Please sir, I have not done my homework".

Dr. Charles Hill, Ascension Day dinner of Worshipful Company of Parish Clerks, Innholders Hall, City of London, May 18, 1950:

A doctor, a lawyer and a parson were shipwrecked on a desert island and the only chance of survival was for one of them to swim for help through a shark-infested sea. They drew lots and the lawyer lost. He set out with the other two watching him. Hundreds of sharks appeared but instead of attacking him they lined up on either side of him as an escort. The parson said it was a miracle and an answer to his prayers. The doctor observed: "It is merely an example of professional courtesy".

Lord Justice Birkett, Saints and Sinners Club dinner, Dorchester Hotel, April 12, 1954:

I have come to the conclusion that the best method of telling stories is the one adopted by members of the Irish Bar. They had a room set apart at the Law Courts and a number would sit there and rock and roar with laughter. One could see the most extraordinary thing happening. One of them would call out a number, say number 4, and all would begin to laugh. Another member would call out, say number 8, and they would all go off into peals of laughter. But whenever anyone called out the number 13 there was no laughter, only silence. Any other number could be called and more laughter would follow. Asked what the explanation was I was told they were all very old friends of many years standing and they all knew each others stories. They had numbered all the stories and instead of retelling each they would just call out the number given to each one. Asked why no one laughed when the number 13 was called I was told, "He tells them so badly".

Frank Shires, president of Food Manufacturer's Federation at Institute of Meat dinner, Innholder's Hall, City of London, April 28, 1952:

A farmer had a valuable cow that mysteriously went sick and he asked the advice of another farmer. The friend said he had given Spirits of Turpentine to his cow when she went sick. The farmer thanked him and gave his sick cow a good strong dose of Spirits of Turpentine. The cow died. The farmer complained to his friend, who replied: "That is strange, so did mine".

Lord De L'Isle and Dudley, V.C. Air Minister, at dinner of British Antique Dealers' Association at Grosvenor House, May 19, 1954:

A man went to an auction to buy a valuable parrot he badly wanted. He thought of bidding up to £36. The bidding went up to £105 before it was knocked down to him. Afterwards he asked the auctioneer who was the other man who kept bidding against him. "That wasn't another man; that was the parrot you bought" replied the auctioneer.

Mr. S.C. Bond, chairman of the association of Traders Road Transport Association Ltd, Grosvenor House, May 27, 1954:

Statistics can be very misleading. A survey was taken at colleges of men and women in America with the object of ascertaining whether the men graduates had more children than the women graduates. It was found that men had one decimal eight children and the women graduates had one decimal four children. The conclusion drawn was that men had more children than women.

Sir Ashley Clarke, Former Ambassador in Russia, at Golden Jubilee dinner of Performing Rights Society, Dorchester Hotel, June 26, 1964:

The commandant of a Prisoner-of-War camp in Germany during the war knew that an escape tunnel was being constructed but had no idea where. He called the British leaders together and told them: "You think I known damn nothing about the tunnel you are making. But you are mistaken. I know damn all."

An elderly French lady was very fond of Beethoven. Every evening she would do her best to play a few pages of her favourite composer. And every night, on her knees before going to bed, she would be heard to say: "Sorry Beethoven".

Mr. C. Naunton Morgan, vice president of the Royal College of Surgeons at Buckston Browne dinner of the College, July 8, 1964:

A phrase in English was fed into a computer in Moscow: "The spirit is willing but the flesh is weak". When it came out in Russian it was fed back and translated into English. The translation was: "The vodka is good but the meat is bad".

Lord De Lisle and Dudley, V.C. Air Minister, at British Antique Dealers' Association dinner, Grosvenor House, May 19, 1954:

Speaking into the microphone, he said: "I have never recovered from my feelings towards this rather sinister looking instrument. I was fortunate — or unfortunate enough to address a luncheon club and I told what I thought was a very witty story. Not a muscle on the faces of any of the diners moved. I asked the Master of Ceremonies if the microphone and loud-speakers were working and I am afraid he answered that they were".

Lord Justice Norman Birkett, Saints and Sinners Club dinner Dorchester Hotel, April 12, 1954:

In New York I heard a speaker say: "If you get up earlier than your neighbour and scheme more and plan more and work harder getting ahead and stay up longer, you will get ahead of your neighbour. When you come to die you will have lived a lot more than he has — and you will leave it a hell of a lot sooner".

Col. H. Randal Steward, president, Institute of Refrigeration, Grosvenor House, January 27, 1965:

An Englishman who could not speak French found himself at a table in a Paris hotel with a Frenchman who could not speak English. "Bon appetite" remarked the Frenchman as they sat down together. Thinking the Frenchman was announcing his name, he replied "Robinson". There was no other conversation during the meal. This went on for several mornings. Mr. Robinson happened to mention this Mr. Bon Appetite to the hotel manager in casual conversation, who told him that was not the Frenchman's name but that he was wishing him a pleasant breakfast. The next morning Mr. Robinson was the first to say Bon Appetite. And the Frenchman gravely replied "Robinson".

Sir Milner Holland, Q.C. at dinner of Royal Institution of Chartered Surveyors, Grosvenor House, March 6, 1962:

Bernard Shaw sent a letter to Winston Churchill enclosing two tickets for the first night of his play Candida and wrote: "I enclose two tickets, one for yourself and one for your friend — if you have one". Churchill replied: "Dear Shaw, thank you very much but I cannot use those two tickets for your first night. But I would like two for your second night — if you have one."

Mr. B.J. Collins, secretary of the Commission for New Towns, at Royal Institution of Chartered Surveyors dinner, Grosvenor House, March 6, 1962:

The new towns are acquiring a population problem. I have no doubt the tenants and house owners will keep the wolf from the door but the trouble is the stork flies in through the window.

Mr. B.J. Collins, secretary of Commission on New Towns, at dinner of Royal Institution of Chartered Surveyors, Grosvenor House, March 6, 1962:

I spoke to a cute little girl the other day and told her: "I hear God has sent you two little twin brothers." "Yes", she replied. "And what is more He knows where their school fees are coming from."

I heard a waiter ask a diner at a dinner the other night: "Will you have red or white wine, sir?" The diner replied: "It doesn't matter to me at all — I'm colour blind".

Sir Howard Florey, President of Royal Society at dinner of Royal Institution of Naval Architects, Grosvenor House, March 24, 1965:

An Englishman on holiday in Paris sat at a table outside a cafe near the Place de l'Opera and a Frenchman came and sat at the same table. A fly alighted on his cup, and the Englishman, to show off his French, remarked: "Voici le mouche". The Frenchman glanced at the fly and replied quietly: "La mouche, monsieur"! The Englishmen answered: "My God, I didn't think anyone had such good eyesight".

Minister of Health, Mr. Anthony Barber, dinner of National Association of State Enrolled Nurses, at House of Lords, April 21, 1964:

A woman driving a rear-engined car for the first time along a motor-way broke down and on opening the bonnet found no engine there. She waved down another motorist who turned out to be a woman with a similar type of car. The first woman said: "It's extraordinary, but I've lost my engine". The second woman replied: "That's alright, because by a coincidence I find I've got a spare in my boot".

Mr. J.M. Laing, president of British Employer's Confederation, and president designate of Confederation of British Industries, at dinner of Federation of Civil Engineering Contractors, Dorchester Hotel, May 11, 1965:

I have recently returned from a tour of Russia with delegates from the industry. One of the members took a crash course of Russian in twelve lessons. It was unfortunately given by a Russian who could not speak English. Our member had to make a speech in Georgia and as he rose to his feet he suddenly forgot what was the Russian for Ladies and Gentlemen. But he noticed two doors in front of him across the dining room and he began his speech. It was received with mystified smiles but not with great fervour. Afterwards he asked a gentleman sitting on his right how the speech had gone down. The neighbour confided: "In Russia we normally start our speeches with the words "Ladies and Gentlemen" and not with "Water Closets and Urinals".

GENERAL

Mr. J.M. Laing, president of British Employers Confederation, at dinner of Federation of Civil Engineering Contractors, Dorchester Hotel, May 11, 1965:

General de Gaulle opened an exhibition of paintings in Paris and was escorted round by the director. He looked at several pieces and stopped in front of one said: "Ah, that is a Monier". "No", replied the director "that is a Renoir". General de Gaulle, without replying, moved on and then stopped again. He remained motionless for several seconds and then observed: "But that is a Picasso". "No", answered the director, "that is a mirroir".

Lord Westwood, director of Lombank, at dinner of Finance House Association, Savoy Hotel, May 18, 1965:

There is always someone in a golf club who is a nark, always complaining about the state of the fairway, the rough and the tee. One of these at a well-known golf club suddenly collapsed and was taken to hospital dangerously ill. The secretary was asked to write to him and wish him a speedy recovery. The secretary wrote: "Dear Sir, I reported to the committee that you had been taken ill and I was instructed by the committee to write to you on behalf of it and wish you a long convalescence. This resolution was passed 5 and 4."

Cardinal Godfrey, Archbishop of Westminster, addressing International dinner of Catholic doctors, Dorchester Hotel, 1962:

A company director, addressing his board, said: ". . . Those are my principles, gentlemen — but if you cannot accept them, I have others".

Sir Edward Thompson, President, at London Central Board Licensed Victuallers dinner, Connaught Rooms, 1967:

I am reminded of the story about the African chieftain whose tribe had always been warring against neighbouring tribes. On his return from the London School of Economics he got in touch with the chief of another tribe and said: "Come and dine with me and bring your cabinet and we will settle the matter between us". The invitation was accepted and they came to dine. They had drinks before dinner and about halfway through the dinner one chief said to the other, (who had also been to the London School of Economics); "You know this is much more sensible than killing each other. We have no differences now, and if any differences arise, we must do this again and it won't be necessary to kill anyone". After a while, the other chap said: "My dear fellow, I entirely agree this is a much better way". He then said: "I don't want to start the war again, and I don't want in any way to be offensive but I am bound to tell you that I don't like your wife." The reply was: "My dear chap, please don't worry about that, just eat the potatoes and gravy."

Dr. Charles Hill, Ascension Day dinner of Worshipful Company of Parish Clerks, Innholders Hall, City of London, May 18, 1950:

A Parliamentary candidate made an inspiring speech at an election meeting and at its conclusion sat down amidst a burst of cheering. When it had died down, a member of the audience rose and shouted: "How much were you paid to give that speech?" "Nothing" replied the candidate indignantly. Back came the voice of the interrupter: "and that is just what it is bloody well worth".

Dr. Charles Hill, Minister of Housing & Local Government at a Mansion House dinner, 1962:

A channel tunnel company invited tenders for the construction of a tunnel. One was for fifty three million pounds, another for forty two million and a third for forty thousand pounds. The chairman was intrigued and decided to see the third firm. He went to a small workshop in the East End of London and saw a man, who said "Yes, I can do it. I have all the tackle. I have only one man working for me, my son. I will start on one side and he will start at the other and you will have the tunnel for forty thousand pounds". The chairman asked: "What if you don't meet in the middle?" and the man replied: "Then you will have two tunnels".

LEGAL...
wig
and
gown

Mr. Derek Walker Smith, Q.C. Parliamentary Secretary to Board of Trade, Wholesale Textile Association dinner, Connaught Rooms, February 13, 1956:

The secretary of a wealthy American corporation consulted an eminent lawyer on a complicated trade question. The lawyer gave his answer with the single word "Yes". Shortly afterwards, walking down 5th Avenue the secretary saw the lawyer, to whom he had just paid a very large fee and said "Nice day". Before the lawyer had a chance to reply, the secretary added: "That is a statement, not a question".

Mr. Henry Brooke, Minister of Housing and Local Government, at Incorporated Society of Estate Agents, Dorchester Hotel, November 12, 1959:

A client received his account and thinking it was heavy asked for an itemised break-down. The solicitor's itemised account included: "To recognising you in the street and crossing the busy road to talk to you to discuss your affairs and recrossing the road after discovering it was not you".

Two married people could not get on because of husband's income and wife's patability.

Lord Kilmuir, Lord Chancellor, Canada Club dinner, Savoy, 1954:

A Permanent Parliamentary Secretary, touring Devon in a car, lost his way and inquired of a stalwart Devonian: "Where am I?" "You are in a car", replied the local. The P.P.S. observed: "That is the perfect answer to a Parliamentary question. It is short, it is true and it does not add one iota to what is known already".

LEGAL

Lord Mayor of London, dinner of Admiralty Court, Guildhall, June 1, 1960:

A man charged with stealing cars was told by the magistrate that he could be tried by his peers or be dealt with by him sitting alone: "What do you mean by peers?" asked the man and was told: "Peers are your equals, men of your own class and own kind". "You try the case on your own", promptly replied the accused, "I don't want to be tried by a bunch of car thieves".

Lord Birkett, Institute of Builders, Guildhall, February 10, 1959:

I have spent more than a little time in after dinner speaking and I am always on the look-out for something that might be fresh. You all know there is no such thing as a really new story. There is a story carried down in all Bar Messes where lawyers meet of the deaf judge, deaf defendant and deaf plaintiff. The judge took his seat, looked at the plaintiff and said: "You begin". The plaintiff said: "My Lord, my claim is for rent". The judge, not having heard a single word, looked at the defendant, and said: "What do you say?" The defendant, also not having heard, said: "My Lord, how can that be so when I grind my corn at night?" The judge retorted: "This is a very difficult problem. I have formed an opinion and I am immensely impressed by the claims. I think she is the mother of both of you and you should both maintain her".

Lord Birkett added: "That story is from Greek mythology and may be 2,000 years old. There are no new stories".

Mr. Ewen Montagu, Q.C. at Allied Brewery Traders Association dinner, Grosvenor House, May 16, 1953:

A judge in America told the assembled court that he had received five thousand dollars by post that morning from the defendant and by the same post he had received three thousand dollars from the plaintiff. He had accordingly returned two thousand dollars to the defendant and so could now try the case without any bias whatever.

Lord Goddard, Lord Chief Justice, at Lord Mayor of London's state banquet to Her Majesty's Judges, Mansion House, July 8, 1954:

Methods of advocacy vary with the countries in which the advocates live. There was the case in Chicago of a beautiful blonde who was promised a mink coat and a Cadillac car but they did not materialise. The man who promised them was shot. The advocate defending her at her trial made a magnificent speech. He said: "There are two possible verdicts in this case. One is guilty and that will mean this lovely woman leaves this court for the death house and the electric chair. The other verdict is Not Guilty. If that is returned it will mean she will leave this court a free woman and return to her lovely comfortable flat on Lake View Avenue — and her telephone number is 2047."

The Lord Mayor of London, Sir Noel V. Bowater, at his State Banquet to Her Majesty's Judges, Mansion House, July 8, 1954:

A young police officer arrested an offender and was asked by him "What is the charge?" The officer replied, "There is no charge, it is all part of my duty".

49

Mr. Ernest Marples, Minister of Transport, at Town Planning Institute dinner, Grosvenor House, March 1, 1964:

In the House of Commons I have a certain view of solicitors. I remember talking to some people from South Africa in Westminster Abbey as they were looking at some monuments of great men. I said to them: "There lies a lawyer and an honest man". One member of the party replied: "Since how long has it been the custom in this country to bury two people in one grave?"

The Lord Mayor of London, Sir Noel Bowater, at his state banquet to Her Majesty's judges, Mansion House, July 8, 1954:

Counsel engaged in a disputed estate case in the High Court were overheard talking together. Said one: "My dear fellow, if we agree to settle, the estate will only be frittered away by the beneficiaries".

The Lord Mayor of London, Sir Noel V. Bowater, at his State Banquet to Her Majesty's Judges, Mansion House, July 8, 1954:

A man about to be sentenced at the Old Bailey for a serious offence who was asked by the clerk of the court if he had anything to say before judgement was passed, replied: "God strike me dead if I am guilty". The judge sat in silence for a moment or two and then addressing the prisoner, said: "Providence not having seen fit to intervene in your case it now becomes my duty to do my humble best to see that justice is done".

Mr. Clifton Webb, High Commissioner for New Zealand, at New Zealand Society dinner, Savoy, February 1957:

A Maori engaged in a legal case was told by his lawyer that it was a case of his word against the other man's and the result would depend on which side the magistrate believed. The lawyer said: "If he believes your story, you win, but if he believes the other man's, he wins. It will depend upon your demeanour in the witness box". The Maori asked: "Will it help if I send the old beak along a brace of pheasants?" The lawyer answered: "If you do that it will be the end of your case". The Maori won his case and afterwards told the lawyer: "The brace of pheasants did the trick." The horrified lawyer cried: "Don't tell me you sent him a brace of pheasants?". And the Maori answered: "Yes, I sent them in the other man's name".

Cardinal Godfrey, Archbishop of Westminster at International Conference dinner to Catholic Doctors, Dorchester Hotel, 1962:

The difference between a lawyer and a surgeon is that a lawyer is always concerned with leaving nothing out and a surgeon is always concerned with leaving nothing in.

The Lord Mayor of London, Sir Frederick Hoare at a Mansion House dinner, 1962:

The last time I was at the Old Bailey I listened with great interest to an Irish labourer being cross-examined. Finally the judge asked his counsel: "Has your client never heard of the well-established doctrine 'Quamdiu se bene gesserit'?" Counsel replied: "With great respect, my Lord, when the boys gather on a Saturday night on the bogs of Ireland they talk of nothing else".

*Lord Justice Diplock, at dinner of Chartered Auctioneers &
Estate Agents Institute, 1965:*

Some 80 years ago the Royal Courts of Justice were being
opened by Queen Victoria and it became necessary that a little
address should be presented to her on behalf of Her Majesty's
Judges. A small address committee was formed and eventually the
proposed address began: "Conscious as we are of our own
deficiencies . . ." One judge demurred and the problem was solved
when it was agreed the address should begin: "Conscious as we are
of one another's deficiencies . . .".

*Lord Justice Diplock, at dinner of Chartered Accountants &
Estate Agents Institute, 1965:*

A man, called into the jury box at the opening of a trial was
about to take the oath when he asked to be excused, saying: "My
wife is due to conceive this afternoon and I would like to be
there". Mr. Justice Cassels turned to him and said: "I think you
have got that wrong. You may mean that your wife is about to be
delivered of a child. But whether I am right or you are right I
certainly think you should be there."

*Mr. G.D. Roberts, Q.C. at Saints and Sinners Club dinner,
Dorchester Hotel, April 12, 1954:*

Given a man and a woman staying at the same hotel, signing as
Mr. and Mrs. —, staying in the same room and sleeping in the same
bed, the law presumes there was intimacy — unless they are
husband and wife.

Sir Godfrey Russell Vick, Q.C. at Traders Road Transport Association Ltd. dinner, Grosvenor House, May 27, 1954:

A fellow was driving along a country lane in a pony and trap when there was a collision with a motorist. The pony and trap was overturned into a ditch. The fellow claimed damages and there was a sequel in court against the motorist. Cross examination of the fellow went like this:

Counsel for the motorist: Is it not right that after the accident you told the motorist that you were alright?

Pony driver: That is difficult to answer.

Counsel: Surely you can answer yes or no to that simple question?

The Judge wisely intervened saying: Tell the court what happened.

The pony driver: Well, the motorist hit me and drove on. He came back and found the pony in the ditch. He said: 'Poor beast, he has two broken legs' and pulled out a gun and shot it dead. Then he turned to me and asked me if I was alright. I said I was.

Sir Godfrey Russell Vick, Q.C. at Traders Road Transport Association Ltd. dinner, Grosvenor House, May 27, 1954:

A jury in a criminal court retired to consider their verdict. They returned in an hour and asked the judge whether the prisoner had chosen his counsel himself or whether he had been appointed by the court. The judge, puzzled, said the accused had chosen his counsel himself. The foreman then turned round and looked at the rest of the jury, all of whom nodded their heads. "We find the prisoner insane", he told the judge.

Sir Godfrey Russell Vick, Q.C. at dinner of Traders Road Transport Association Ltd., Grosvenor House, May 27, 1954:

A case was ending concerning a public nuisance. After a very long and tedious summing up by the learned judge the jury retired, returned to court and found the defendant guilty. The foreman added: "The jury would like to thank your Lordship very much because it was not until we heard your long summing-up that we knew what a public nuisance was".

Lord Birkett, Saints and Sinners Club, Dorchester, March 23, 1959:

A prisoner was acquitted and asked for costs. He said he knew he was innocent because he was in prison at the time. Asked why he did not say this during his trial, the man replied: "I thought it might prejudice my case".

RELIGION...
clerical
error

Lord Birkett, dinner of Saints and Sinners, Dorchester Hotel, February 27, 1961:

An archbishop, before flying to New York, was warned to be very careful about what he said to reporters. On arriving at New York he was interviewed by the press and he was asked about his plans and the purpose of his visit. Then one reporter asked him: "What do you think of the brothels on the East Side of New York?" The archbishop, remembering how cautious he had to be, in a non-committal way, asked: "Are there brothels on the East Side of New York?" The next morning, to his horror, he saw his photograph in a newspaper with the headline: "Archbishop's first question: 'Are there brothels on the East Side of New York?' "

Lord Alexander of Tunis, dinner of Institution of Municipal Engineers, Dorchester Hotel, January 29, 1954:

I feel like the curate newly appointed to a parish who on his first Sunday found the vicar was ill and had to take the service. Mounting the steps to the pulpit to give his first sermon, he began: "My dearly beloved brethren, I must apologise owing to the illness of our vicar, but I have had no time to prepare a sermon. Therefore I can only say the words that God puts into my mouth. Next week I hope to say something much more worthy".

Lord Mancroft, Saints and Sinners Club, Dorchester Hotel, April 4, 1955:

I am strictly a middle of the road man — I have one foot firmly on the primrose path and the other jammed in the Pearly Gates. I subscribe to the view of the old lady who, when in church, always bowed her head when the devil was mentioned. On being asked why, she replied: "You never know. It might come in handy".

Dr. Charles Hill, at National Federation of Building Trades Employers dinner, Grosvenor House, February 6, 1962:

A man short of ten million pounds for a deal decided to go to church to pray and get a little bit of help. By a coincidence he was joined as he knelt by a man who owed another £25. The man owing the money was praying aloud for a miracle. The first man heard the appeal to the Almighty and putting his hand in his pocket took out £25 and pressed it into the other man's hand. Overjoyed, the second man left. Then the big business man, returning to his own appeal, prayed: "Now, please Almighty, may I have your undivided attention".

Lord Birkett, dinner of Saints and Sinners, Dorchester Hotel, February 27, 1961:

In the days when the Foreign Office had some control over the monks of Mount Athos a telegram was sent to the F.O. "The monks of Mount Athos have violated their vows". By some mischance Lord Curzon read the telegram as "The monks of Mount Athos have violated their cows". Someone had written across it: "No doubt caused by a Papal Bull". Lord Curzon wrote: "A mere clerical error".

Lord Mayor of London, Ald. Cuthbert Ackroyd, at Lord Mayor's state dinner to Archbishops and Bishops, Mansion House, June 21, 1956:

A curate was called on at the last moment to deputise for the bishop. The Cathedral was crowded and the curate was nervous. Afterwards, in the vestry, he apologised to the vicar's warden for his inadequate sermon. The vicar's warden replied: "Don't worry, you did your best. It's those who sent you who should be shot".

Mr. Geoffrey D. Blake, President of Chartered Auctioneers and Estate Agents Institution, Dorchester Hotel, June 28, 1956:

A clergyman was very reluctant to go into the pulpit and give a sermon. He was persuaded by his warden that he had to and one Sunday he climbed up into the pulpit and asked the congregation if they knew what he was going to say. They replied "No". He answered: "Neither do I" and left the pulpit. The following Sunday, under pressure, he again went into the pulpit. "Do you know what I am going to say?", he again asked. The congregation, remembering what had happened the previous Sunday, answered "Yes". "Then you do not need me to say it", said the vicar and left the pulpit. The next Sunday he asked the same question. Some members of the congregation being confused answered "Yes" and others answered "No". Whereupon the vicar told them: "Well, if those who answered "Yes" will tell those who answered "No", there will be no need for me to tell them."

Rear-Admiral G. Thistleton-Smith, Admiral Commanding Reserves, R.N.V.R. reunion dinner, Connaught Rooms, Oct. 19, 1956:

It is said God helps those who help themselves. A bishop, the other day, visited a beautiful garden and found, in the greenhouse, the gardener preparing the plants for later planting out. "What a wonderful work can be effected with God and a gardener working together", he said. "Oh ar", replied the gardener, "but you should have seen it before I took over and God had it on his own".

Charles Chaplin, at Dickens Fellowship dinner, Cafe Royal, February 7, 1955:

A widow, with her little boy, attended the funeral service of her husband. The minister extolled his virtues, describing what a wonderful man he was, what a kind and generous father, and what a fine sober, home-loving and ideal family man. The widow turned to her little boy and whispered: "Let's go, son. We have come to the wrong funeral".

Lord Mayor of London, Sir Seymour Howard, dinner of the Institute of Chartered Accountants, Guildhall, May 9, 1955:

Sometime ago a distinguished cleric journeyed to a distant church to take a service and was met by the vicar, who asked him: "As you have had a long journey may I offer you a little liquid refreshment?" The cleric replied: "No thank you for three reasons. The first is I am just about to take Divine service; the second is I happen to be the president of the local temperance association; and the third is I have just had one."

Mr. C.J. Howell, member of the council of Chartered Institute of Secretaries, at their dinner, Guildhall, December 8, 1959:

A stock-broker died and reached St. Peter, who wanted to know what he had done to justify his entrance to Heaven. The stock-broker said that two or three weeks ago he had given two shillings to an old flower-seller he had seen in Throgmorton Street and that last week he had given a shilling to a newsagent. St. Peter told the recording angel: "Give him his three bob back and tell him to go to hell."

Mr. Derek Walker Smith, Minister of State, Board of Trade, Association of Consulting Engineers, Dorchester Hotel, February 18, 1957:

The bishop went to hear the first sermon of a newly appointed vicar, the Rev. Mr. Smith. During the sermon, the vicar told the congregation: "The happiest days of my life have been spent in the arms of another man's wife . . ." There was an electric shock throughout the congregation which only relaxed and smiled when he added, after a suitable pause, ". . . In the arms of my mother".

The bishop was very impressed and decided to incorporate it in his next sermon. In his cathedral he began his sermon: "The happiest days of my life have been spent in the arms of another man's wife". Again there was the reaction of shock from the congregation. The old bishop paused and then stuttered, in confusion, "But I can't remember who".

Julian Amery, Parliamentary Under Secretary of State for Colonies, Royal College of Surgeons, July 3, 1960:

The sun was setting in the Coliseum a hundred years after the birth of Christ and Caesar was in the Imperial Lodge. A Christian was pushed into the arena and then a ferocious lion rushed in and knocked him down. It was about to devour him when he whispered in the lion's ear and after that the animal would not go near him. It was taken away and another lion was brought in. The same thing happened, and again with a third lion. Caesar called him and told him: "I will spare your life if you tell me what you told the lion". The Christian answered: "I whispered, 'Beware, you will have to make a speech after your dinner.' "

Sir Roger Duncalfe, President of Organisation for International Standardisation, at a dinner of Chartered Quantity Surveyors, Grosvenor House, November 20, 1956:

Two bishops went to the gates of Heaven and were met by St. Peter with courtesy but without any sign of enthusiasm. He asked them to wait in a room for a few minutes. While waiting a glamorous blonde arrived and was also asked to wait. She whispered in his ear and he immediately took her right through the gates and to the land beyond. The bishops felt embarrassed at the beauty being given preferential treatment and complained to St. Peter. St. Peter replied: "That woman's husband gave her a new car six months ago. In that time she has put the fear of God into more people than you have in the whole of your lives".

Mr. Henry Brooke, Minister of Local Government, Institution of Municipal Engineers, Hyde Park Hotel, March 10, 1960:

A minister of religion wrote to the borough engineer of his town: "On leaving the vicarage this morning I saw a dead dog in the gutter. Please remove the carcass". The borough engineer replied, not pleased: "I invite your attention to Holy Scripture wherein it is written: 'Let the dead bury their dead' ". He received the reply from the vicar: "I do not need the assistance of a borough engineer to instruct me in Holy Writ. The reason I wrote to you was because I was acting on the precept: 'The first duty of a citizen in any case of sudden death is to inform the next of kin' ".

Lord Aberdare, Coal Trade Benevolent Association, Connaught Rooms, December 7, 1959:

King David and King Solomon lived merry merry lives
They had many many lady friends and many many wives.
But when old age crept upon them
With many many qualms
King Solomon wrote the proverbs and King David wrote the Psalms.

Lord Boothby, Anglo-Israel Association, Mayfair Hotel, November 24, 1958:

Lady Bonham-Carter was with me in Israel and we went to the Church of the Beatitudes on the site of which the Sermon on the Mount was alleged to have been preached. Lady Bonham-Carter became rather cross and said rather primly: "I am quite certain the Sermon on the Mount was not preached here". She walked over to the porch where I asked her where she thought it had been preached. She pointed and said: "I think it was preached over there". Our Israeli guide remarked: "Well, Lady Bonham-Carter, you can have it where you like, it is your religion".

Mr. Lewis Douglas, American Ambassador, at Australian Club dinner, Savoy Hotel, 1950:

There is the famous story of an American political meeting in 1932 when a speaker at a Republican rally concluded his appeal for assistance with the words: "Oh God, I call upon you to come down from above and help our cause. But, O God if you are not able to come down yourself do not send your son Jesus Christ because this is no child's play."

Mr. Roy Thomson, newspaper proprietor, at Institute of Public Relations dinner, Mansion House, 1962:

A young lad in the highlands of Scotland got a secretarial job in London. His parents had heard of the great temptations befalling those in that great wicked city. They admonished him at great length and told him: "You must never forget your strict Presbyterian principles and upbringing." They called in the minister and he told the lad the same thing. "You must never forget your strict Presbyterian principles". The lad asked him: "Will the strict Presbyterian principles protect me from these temptations?" The minister replied: "No, but they will stop you from enjoying them".

Sir Alec Douglas-Home, at dinner of Royal Scottish Corporation, 1965:

There are great risks in extemporaneous speaking, risks I have always been conscious of since I heard a story. It was about the curate who gave his first sermon. He was a very shy man and he got into such a state before the service began that he took a glass of sherry to steady his nerves. He had never taken alcohol before. Feeling much better he climbed up into the pulpit, crushed up his notes and preached from the heart — in simple words and with conviction. After the service, in the vestry, he asked the vicar: "How did I do?" The vicar replied: "Considering it was your first sermon it was really a remarkable performance. But there are three things I would like to point out: first it was the Philistines and not the Americans whom the Israelites defeated; secondly it was David who slew Goliath and not the other way round; and thirdly please remember it was a small pebble that David used and not a bloody great rock."

Mr. Arthur G. Coombe, past president of National Association of Furniture Warehousemen & Removers, at Jubilee dinner, Park Lane Hotel, May 3, 1950:

A Roman Catholic priest and a Church of England clergyman were arguing about religion. They both became rather heated and then the priest said: "We must not quarrel. We are both doing God's work — you in your way and I in His".

Lord Mayor of London, Sir Leslie Boyce, at dinner of the Worshipful Company of the Art and Mystery of Gold and Silver Wyre Drawers, Mansion House, November 5, 1952:

Although your long looked-for charter was not acquired until William and Mary granted it in 1693, yours is a very ancient, interesting and elegant craft. We are told in the Book of Exodus that Moses used it in the making of the Ephod or priestly vestments. But if I were you I would not believe everything you read about Moses. In this respect I am reminded of the verse:

The Pharaoh had a daughter
With a most bewitching smile.
She saw a lovely boy one day
While bathing in the Nile.
She took it to her mother
And said she found it by the shore.
"Alas, my dear," the old girl said,
"I've heard that tale before".

Dr. Coggan, Archbishop of York at Lord Mayor of London's state banquet to Archbishops & Bishops, 1965:

A Yorkshireman, who had been celebrating a little too much in London, lurched unsteadily down one of the narrow streets and saw advancing towards him the black forms of two nuns. As they approached they parted to make a safe passage for him. He reached the support of a lamp-post and leaning against it, was heard to remark: "How in the world did she do it?"

Lord Mayor of London, Sir Frederick Hoare, at Livery dinner of Worshipful Company of Farmers, Mansion House, January 22, 1961:

A Quaker farmer had a temperamental cow who would keep kicking over the milk bucket as soon as it was half full. At last it proved too much for him and he told the cow: "Thou knows't I am a Quaker and so I cans't beat thee. But what thou doest not know is that tomorrow I am going to sell thee to a Baptist — and then God help thee".

Lord Mayor of London, Sir Frederick Hoare, at Lord Mayor's dinner to Court of Common Council, Mansion House, January 25, 1961:

I have great admiration for the bishop who was noted for the brevity of his sermons and conversation. On one occasion he was entertained by the Mayoress of his home town. She tried in vain to hold a conversation with His Lordship but gave up in despair. Finally the conversation was: "Some tea, bishop?" "No tea". "Some coffee, bishop?" "No coffee". "Some whisky and soda, bishop?" "No soda".

Bishop of Bath and Wells, Society of Yorkshiremen in London, Dorchester Hotel, November 12, 1953:

Explained how his title became Bishop of Bath AND Wells: Early in the 12th century a cleric of Wells was approached by the king and asked whether, in return for his valuable service, he would like to become the Bishop of Bath or the Bishop of Wells. In his broad Somerset dialect, the cleric replied "Bishop of Bath'. 'Very well' observed the King, misunderstanding the accent, 'Both it shall be".

Sir Thomas White, High Commissioner of Australia, at Institute of Transport dinner, Grosvenor House, February 27, 1954:

Speaking of British tradition, he said it had been known for men to sit for months and months opposite each other in a train and not exchange a word. "I do not believe in that", he said. "Two Englishmen, I have been told, were antagonistic towards each other as schoolboys. When they grew up one became a general and the other a bishop. They found themselves sitting opposite each other in an otherwise empty compartment of a train. The bishop wanted to know when to alight and asked the general 'Admiral, can you tell me the name of the next station?' The general, glancing at the bishop's apron, replied: 'Madam, I do not know'.

Col. H. Randal Steward, president, Institution of Refrigeration, Grosvenor House, January 27, 1965:

A clergyman, while flying to America, was asked by the hostess if he would like some refreshment. He asked for a whisky and ginger ale. While it was being brought the pilot announced that they were flying at 40,000 ft. When the drink arrived he accepted only the ginger ale and declined the whisky. Asked by the hostess why, he replied: "I am getting a bit near my head office".

Air Marshal Sir Herbert Spreckley, Electrical Engineers Exhibition dinner, Grosvenor House, September 28, 1961:

A curate was going to give his first sermon in a village and the vicar asked him what his text would be. The curate replied: "The widow's mite". The vicar observed: "There are only two widows in the village and they both do".

The Archbishop of Canterbury, Dr. Ramsay, at dinner of Council of Christians and Jews, Mansion House, October 12, 1961:

I hope you know the classic story of harmony and disharmony. A clergyman was conducting a wedding and the groom had his prayer book open at the wrong page. The clergyman asked him: "Wilt thou take this woman to be thy wedded wife?" and the nervous groom replied: "I will renounce the Lord". The clergyman, getting exasperated, told him: "If you behave like this I will have you turned out", and the groom's response was: "That is my desire".

Mr. George Brown, Shadow Cabinet Home Secretary, at Middlesex County dinner, Grosvenor House, January 12, 1962:

One of the notable dinners I have attended was one with Kruschev. Later, someone told me he had died, and on going to Heaven had a somewhat difficult reception. Peter was not sure what to do and was non-plussed. He asked Kruschev to wait in the waiting room and went to see the All Highest. The All Highest told Peter: "We never turn anyone away from here. Let him in but explain he is on a year's probation and tell him that a condition of his probation is that he must not make any speeches and must not chuck his weight about". Peter explained this to Kruschev who agreed to the conditions. A year later Peter went back to the All Highest with his report. The All Highest asked him if Kruschev had made any speeches or thrown his weight about and Peter replied: "No comrade".

SEXES
& KINDRED
SUBJECTS...
the
age~old
topic

Sir Eric Harrison, High Commissioner for Australia, at Australia Club dinner, Dorchester Hotel, February 1, 1960:

An American negro on a plantation produced a new baby every year, and each time, the master gave him a dollar. When his family came to twelve babies the master told him: "Look here, Sambo, this is enough of this baby business. I have no more dollars. You ought to be ashamed of yourself and if you do it again you ought to hang yourself". In due course the thirteenth baby arrived. Sambo got a rope, went out into the bush and put it round the limb of a tree. He put the noose round his neck and was about to hang himself when he thought: "Be careful Sambo, you might be hanging the wrong man".

Mr. A. Dickson Wright, F.R.C.S. at dinner of Saints and Sinners, Dorchester Hotel, February 27, 1961:

Two old Chelsea pensioners were talking about their gay old days. One, aged 70, asked: "Do you remember the pills they gave us in the Boer war to diminish our activities?" and the other aged 86 replied: "Yes, they are just beginning to work".

Lord Mancroft, at Buyers Benevolent Association dinner, Grosvenor House, March 9, 1954:

Like King Solomon, when confronted by an enterprising buyer who showed him 271 new wives in a new harem, he knew perfectly well what was expected of him but did not quite know where to begin. I am in the same position.

Lord Jowett, the Lord Chancellor, Canada Club, Savoy Hotel, July 1, 1949:

A master was taking students in ethics and Scripture. He asked if they would prefer to be with the ten Wise Virgins with the light, or the unwise Virgins in the dark — and he was surprised at the unanimous answer.

Mr. Ewen Montagu, Q.C. at Allied Brewery Traders Association dinner, Grosvenor House, March 16, 1953:

A company director had to take his pretty secretary on a business tour and at one hotel they stopped at late at night there was only one room available. He asked her if she would object to sharing the room with him, to which she replied "No, I have complete trust in you". They shared the one bed and shortly after getting into it she asked, "Would you mind getting me a glass of water?" He countered, "I was about to ask you a question. Would you like me to imagine you are my wife?" Demurely she replied that she would, whereupon he roared out: "Well, bloody well get it yourself".

Sir Herbert Williams, M.P., President of Ballast, Sand and Allied Trades Association, at their banquet, Grosvenor House, March 16, 1954:

I don't quite know what a good citizen is. There is the story of the young man walking along the street who saw a beautiful blonde. As they drew level he said to her: "Gentlemen prefer blondes". She replied: "And blondes prefer gentlemen. Good night".

Major-General G.W. Duke, Engineer-in-Charge, Army Institute of Refrigeration, Grosvenor House, January 27, 1965:

A distinguished judge had had a busy day in the Divorce Court and returning to his room, sat down in a comfortable chair and remarked to his clerk: "I never slept with my wife before I married her. Did you?" The clerk, all flummuxed, replied: "I can't really say, my lord. What was her maiden name?"

Mayor of Wandsworth, Councillor Leslie Farmiloe, dinner of Federation of Painting Contractors, Dorchester Hotel, March 2, 1964:

George Bernard Shaw was asked at a dinner to give his observations on sex. He rose and said: "Ladies and Gentlemen, it gives me great pleasure", and resumed his seat.

Lord Amory, former Chancellor of the Exchequer, Saints and Sinners dinner, Dorchester Hotel, April 13, 1964:

A young man hesitated during his 21st birthday speech and afterwards asked his mother: "Mother, why is it I am so shy and you are not?" She replied: "It is because you take after your father. If he had not been so shy you would now have been celebrating your 22nd birthday".

Mr. P.H.R. Turner, chairman, Road Haulage Association (Met. & S.E. area), Grosvenor House, March 12, 1962:

A lorry driver, travelling down an arterial road at night, saw a glamorous blonde standing by the roadside flagging him down. She was dressed in a fur coat and this so surprised him that he stopped. "Can I give you a lift?", he asked. "I would not if I were you. I am a witch", she replied. He smiled and said: "I'll take a chance". She climbed in beside him and they set off. After several miles she touched him on the knee and he turned into a lay-by.

Mr. Brian Eve, member of council, dinner of Royal Institution of Chartered Surveyors, Grosvenor House, March 5, 1963:

To tell the difference between a woman barrister and a woman solicitor is quite easy. To take a simple illustration: a woman barrister is one who has briefs. If she doesn't have briefs she is more probably a solicitor.

Earl Mountbatten of Burma, Conference of the Electronics Industry dinner, Dorchester Hotel, November 10, 1964:

This is a true story so far as I know. A young man would not settle down and marry. His parents told him: "You must find yourself a suitable girl and marry her". After a couple of months he told them he had proposed to and been accepted by a charming girl. His mother was over-joyed, but his father, on hearing who the girl was, forbade the marriage. The father refused to give his reason until the son said he would marry the girl unless a reason was given why he should not. The father then told him: "You can't marry her because she is your half-sister". The son, very upset, told his mother. She told him: "That's alright, son. You go ahead. You don't have to worry because he is not your father."

Mr. John Boyd Carpenter, Minister of Pensions, dinner of Association of British Aero Clubs and Centres, Waldorf Hotel, February 17, 1956:

A man of parsimonious tendency was in a public house and had several rounds without offering to buy one himself. When the time for him to buy a round was forced upon him, he started to leave, saying: "I'm sorry the only money I've got in my pocket is my wife's maternity benefit". One of his mates observed: "You are so mean you would not even have had that but for me".

Mr. W. Charles Norton, President of the Law Society, dinner of Building Societies Institute, Hyde Park Hotel, March 8, 1956:

I feel somewhat like that officer, who, during the war, found himself quartered in a building formerly used as a girls' school. When he retired for the night, he found a notice above his bed: "If during the night you require a mistress ring the bell".

An advertisement appeared in a county newspaper in relation to property for sale: "One of the unusual features of the residence is the batchelor's apartments with the private bath. The maids' bedrooms are conveniently situated and are reached by a private staircase".

An advertisement appeared in a local newspaper at a naval port for a housekeeper, and finished: "Suitable for married couple or naval officer and his wife".

Dr. Charles Hill, Post-Master General, dinner of London Chamber of Commerce, Grosvenor House, September 4, 1956:

In Brighton it was Brenda,
It was Patsy up in Perth,
In Cambridge she was Clarissa,
The sweetest thing on earth.
At Stafford she is Stella,
The pick of all the bunch.
But down on his expenses
She is petrol, oil and lunch.

Dr. Charles Hill, Post-Master General, dinner of London Chamber of Commerce, Grosvenor House, September 4, 1956:

A member of the chamber left home one morning to travel to Scotland to discuss a business arrangement, but on getting to his office found that the appointment had been cancelled. He returned home unexpectedly that evening and was settled comfortably in the lounge when the telephone rang. He picked up the receiver, listened to the voice and answered: "This is not the weather-forecasting station. Try the Admiralty". A few moments later, his wife timidly asked him: "Who was that dear?", and he answered: "I don't know; some damn fool asking whether the coast was clear".

Speaker not known: Joint Iron Council dinner, Connaught Rooms, September 24, 1950:

A man met a friend who said he was going to visit his step-wife. When asked what he meant by step-wife, the friend replied: "When the husband steps out I step in".

Mr. Lawrence Abel, vice-president of Royal College of Surgeons, at Hunterian Festival dinner of the College, February 14, 1957:

Explaining the phrase 'Savoir Faire', he gave the example: A husband, returning home unexpectedly, found his wife in the act of being unfaithful. "Pray don't disturb yourself on my account", said the husband to the other man. "Please continue — if you can".

Lord Birkett, Saints and Sinners Club, Dorchester, March 23, 1959:

The electronic machine is a wonderful invention. Trying it out, a man asked it: "Where is my father?" and the machine answered: "Playing golf at St. Andrews". The man laughed and said the machine could not be right as his father died five years ago. The machine interrupted with: "The man married to your mother died five years ago but your father is playing golf at St. Andrews".

David Watson, President of Institution of Municipal Engineers, at their dinner, Hyde Park Hotel, March 10, 1960:

An important guest booked in at the London hotel and in his room beside his bed he found a Gideon Bible. In the fly leaf was written "If you are tired and weary look up Jeremiah 32". Someone had written underneath: "If you are not 'phone Mayfair 111".

Dr. Charles Hill, Chancellor of Duchy of Lancaster, Millinery Trades dinner, Grosvenor House, February 25, 1957:

Two dirty little boys were playing in the street in a London slum when a magnificent Rolls Royce drew up at a dingy little house. The liveried chauffeur opened the door of the car and out stepped a glamorous young woman wearing a fabulously expensive mink coat. "She don't belong here", said one boy, and the other answered: "Yes she does. She's my sister wot's been ruined".

Mr. W.W. Harris, chairman City of London branch, Royal Society of St. George, Mansion House, December 20, 1960:

A guest speaker arrived early at his dinner to rehearse his speech in private. He went into an empty room to go through it. Later, a woman came into the room, recognised him and asked: "I know you are speaking tonight and was wondering if you feel nervous?" "No", he replied, "not at all". The woman observed: "I was just wondering why you were in the ladies' cloak room".

Mrs. Pandit, High Commissioner for India, dinner of Westminster Chamber of Commerce, Park Lane Hotel, November 17, 1960:

A woman went to a hospital and asked a doctor what she could do as she had nine children and could not afford a tenth. He told her: "You must drink a glass of water". She was a little mystified but thanked him and went away. She returned a few moments later and asked: "Shall I drink it before or after?" and the doctor answered "Instead of".

Lord Mancroft, Incorporated Sales Managers Association, Claridge's, February 10, 1960:

When I was at the Ministry of Defence three years ago I attended a banquet at the Painted Hall, Greenwich and I sat next to the wife of a senior officer. She wore a pretty brooch made of miniature naval flags. I asked her what they meant. She said it was a gift from her husband when they were courting and the flags made the signal "I love you". I had some doubt about the flags making that signal and later I spoke to a senior signalling officer. He said: "You are both right. You can't make that signal with flags but there is a similar signal used frequently by ships entering harbour which reads: 'Permission to lay alongside' ".

Mr. S.E. Goodall, President, Institution of Electrical Engineers, Grosvenor House, February 26, 1959:

A salesman was going from door to door trying to sell encyclopedias. At one house a little boy answered the door and told the salesman: "We do not need one because I have just heard my father tell my mother: "I can explain everything".

Lord Thomson of Fleet, dinner in his honour by Thomson organisation, Cafe Royal, May 26, 1964:

A poor farmer of Alberta struck oil and went to Calgary to buy an expensive Cadillac. When he offered cash he was told he would have a discount of 200 dollars. He did not know what a discount was and shortly afterwards, in a cafe, asked a waitress what a discount was. She told him it was "taking off". He asked her: "What would you do for a discount of 200 dollars?" and she answered: "Would my earrings be in your way?"

Lord Thomson of Fleet, at dinner in his honour by Thomson organisation, Cafe Royal, May 26, 1964:

Two clerks in my organisation were talking together. One said: "What do you think of one of our directors. Seeing a clerk about to go home the other night in the rain, he offered the use of his Rolls Royce, took the clerk to his own home, and shared his splendid dinner. The clerk stayed the night and returned in the car to the office the next morning". The other clerk asked: "Did that happen to you?" The clerk answered: "No, but it did to my sister".

Sir Edward Dodd, Chief Inspector of Constabulary, dinner of Traders Road Transport Association, Grosvenor House, April 27, 1964:

A policeman, on night duty, saw a stationary car outside a factory and being suspicious, waited beside it. A man came out shortly afterwards from the main gates and hurried into the car. The officer questioned him and asked him his name and address. The man gave his name as Mr. Cuddlebrake. The officer, not satisfied, decided to check the man's identity. He went to the gatekeeper and asked: "Have you got a Cuddlebrake here?" The gateman replied: "I don't know about that. It has taken us ten years to get a tea break".

Sir Miles Thomas, Chairman of B.O.A.C. at dinner of Association of Supervising Electrical Engineers, Connaught Rooms, April 2, 1954:

Maternity is a matter of fact; paternity is a matter of opinion.

Rear-Admiral R.S. Foster-Brown, dinner of Worshipful Company of Coachmakers & Coach Harness Makers, Guildhall, 1965:

During the war there was a terrible shortage of blue serge for the W.R.N.S. and demands were made to the Admiralty. A high official sent back the signal: "It is quite clear to me the clothes of the W.R.N.S. must be held up until the needs of the sailors are satisfied."

Mr. J.N. Muster, Chairman of the Brewers Society, 1967:

A Scotsman had three sons and used to give them money on their birthdays. The youngest asked for £5 and said he wanted it for a tartan tie. The second asked for £50 and said he wanted it for a tartan kilt. The third asked for £500 and when asked why replied that he had a tartin trouble.

Lord Fraser of Lonsdale at dinner of Chartered Physiotherapists Society 1962:

The custom of a Red Indian tribe was for the chief to give his daughters a bed of skins on being married. A chief had three daughters and each married within the space of a few weeks. The chief presented the first with a bear skin, the second with a moose skin, and the third had a hippopotomus skin. Within a year they all produced children, the last having twins. All this proves that the squaw on the hippotomus is equal to the sex of the squaws on the other two hides."

Sir Edward Dodd, Chief Inspector of Constabulary, dinner of Traders Road Transport Association, Grosvenor House, April 27, 1964:

A Government minister required a new personal secretary and a committee was told to select one. They were looking for one with initiative, enterprise and a knowledge of the world. They advertised in the Civil Service magazine and three were put on the short list. The committee decided to ask them all one question: "If you were cast ashore on a desert island with forty men what would you do?"

The first girl, on being asked, went white and replied: "I would swim and swim and swim". The second girl answered: "I would look around at the forty men and pick the most handsome and strongest. Then I would fling myself into his arms and appeal to him to protect me against the other 39". The third girl simply asked: "I've heard the question. What is the problem?"

Lord Westwood, a director of Lombank, Finance Houses Association dinner, Savoy Hotel, May 18, 1965:

I have a newspaper cutting of a few months ago which says: " 'Stage Romance' and gives the details of a marriage between two stars at a London show. It goes on: "Owing to stage commitments they will have to delay their honeymoon. Both took part in the usual performance last night".

Mr. Bruce B. Kennedy, President of Timber Trades Federation at their dinner, 1965:

Two miners were discussing nationalisation in the early days and one said: "I don't think it is all that it is cracked up to be", and the other replied: "Don't say that. We have worked for this for thirty years and it takes time". "I expect to see something dramatic," was the answer. "Look at those cows in the field", said his friend as they walked through the countryside, "Put a bull amongst them and you would not expect to find a herd of calves the next morning". "No", was the answer, "but I would expect to see a lot of contented faces".

Mr. Charles Pannell, Minister of Public Buildings & Works, at Royal Institution of Chartered Surveyors dinner, 1964:

A judge in an American western town was at home one Saturday night when there was a knock on the door and he saw a soldier with the most beautiful girl in the world. They both asked him to marry them. He told them in that county he could not do it then but he would if they returned on the Monday. They tried to persuade him but by law he was unable to help them. At last the most beautiful girl in the world asked him: "Judge, can't you just say a few words to see us over the week-end?"

Lord Mountbatten of Burma, at dinner of Chartered Auctioneers & Estate Agents Institute, 1965:

The Chinese are a very fecund race and according to statistics printed in a newspaper every fourth child born in the world is Chinese. An Englishwoman, seeing the report, went to her doctor in great distress and asked him: "We have three children and would like a fourth but is it safe if every fourth child is a Chinese?"

MEDICAL...
pills
and people

Mr. Derek Walker Smith, Parliamentary Secretary, Board of Trade, dinner of Wholesale Textile Association, Connaught Rooms February 13, 1956:

A doctor and a politician were having an argument. The politician said: "There are two kinds of doctors — the old family type who lets you die and there is the brilliant young man who kills you off". The doctor retorted: "There are are two kinds of politicians — those who are dead, and those who ought to be".

A call went up on board ship for the urgent help of a doctor. A young lady had fallen and had hurt her leg. He hurried to her cabin only to find he had been beaten by a short head by a doctor of divinity.

Sir Russell Brain, President of the Royal College of Surgeons, dinner of Faculty of Anaesthetists of the Royal College of Surgeons, at the college, March 23, 1955:

A surgeon, an anaesthetist, an architect and a politician were discussing which had the oldest profession. The surgeon claimed resection of Adam's rib took surgery back a long way. The anesthetist pointed out that Adam had to have a deep sleep before he could have been operated upon. The architect said that before that could have been done the heavens and worldly bodies had to be created out of chaos. And the politician then asked: "And who do you think created the chaos?"

Lord Thomson of Fleet at dinner in his honour by Thomson organisation, Cafe Royal, May 26, 1965:

A man went to a doctor because he was feeling ill and thought he was going to die. "What can I do to get well and live to a ripe old age?" he asked. The doctor told him: "Give up drink, tobacco and women and you will live to be a hundred". "Will I really live to be a hundred?" eagerly asked the patient. "No", replied the doctor, "but it will seem like it".

Sir Howard Florey, President of Royal Society, at dinner of Royal Institute of Naval Architects, Grosvenor House, March 24, 1965:

I don't suppose you carry your specialisation very far. A young woman, introduced to a naval surgeon remarked: "Good gracious. I had no conception that surgery had become so specialised."

Sir Cecil Wakeley, President, at Chartered Physiotherapists Society dinner, 1962:

It is extraordinary how the terminology of medical terms has changed. I well remember, when I was a student, long before the first world war, we talked about false teeth. After that war the phrase was never allowed and we had to refer to dentures. The Americans have gone a step further and now call them oral rearmament.

Mr. James E. Currie, Chairman of the American Society in London, at their Independence Day dinner, Dorchester Hotel, July 4, 1961:

The owner of a prosperous business had put on too much weight and went to his doctor to reduce. He was given four pink pills and told to take one each night.

The first night he dreamed of a beautiful young woman. As he moved towards her she moved away. He gave chase and she ran and he could not catch her. The second night he took another pill and had the same dream. He ran about a mile but could not catch her. The third and fourth nights he had the same dream. He would run three or four miles but she always out-ran him. He returned to his doctor and told him about the dreams. The doctor replied "Good, now get on the scales". He had lost 28 lbs and was quite satisfied. He told an employee, also overweight, what had happened. The employee went to the same doctor and was given four black pills. The first night he took a pill he had a dream of the devil chasing him with a sharp three-pronged fork. The next three nights he had the same dream and had to run faster and longer each night to get away from the devil. He returned to the doctor, told him of his dream and found he also had lost 28 lbs. He asked why he dreamt of the devil and his employer dreamt of a beautiful woman. The doctor replied: "You are a panel patient, but your employer is a private patient".

Speaker unknown. Joint Iron Council dinner, Connaught Rooms, September 24, 1950:

A grandfather visited his grandson in hospital and was intrigued by the pills he had been ordered to take. The grandson pointed out that in addition to curing his particular complaint they also had the peculiar effect of intense rejuvenation. The grandfather was very interested and persuaded his grandson to sell him some for a pound, agreeing to pay him the next week when he again visited the hospital. The following week the grandfather duly handed his grandson thirty shillings. Asked what the extra ten shillings were for, the grandfather replied: "A little present from a grateful grandmother".

NATIONAL...
here
and
there

Mr. B.J. Collins, secretary of Commission for New Towns, at Royal Institution of Chartered Surveyors dinner, Grosvenor House, March 6, 1962:

An Englishman walked into a public house in a village in Eire and asked the landlord: "Are you open yet?" "We are not", replied the landlord, "there is half an hour to wait". "Very well I will look around the village while I'm waiting", remarked the Englishman. "Well, now, why would you want to be doing that", asked the landlord. And added: "Why not sit here in comfort and have a drink while you are waiting?"

Sir Sydney Littlewood, former President of the Law Society, president of the Sand and Gravel Association of Great Britain, at annual dinner, Grosvenor House, April 13, 1961:

The Welsh pray on their knees — and on their neighbours;

The Scots keep the Sabbath — and anything else they can lay their hands on;

The Irish don't know what they want and are always prepared to fight to the death to get it; and

The English boast of being a self-made nation — and they thank God for it.

Lord Tenby, at Saints and Sinners dinner, Dorchester Hotel, April 13, 1964:

The Russian wanted to contact a top master spy named Jones in a little Welsh seaside town and sent an agent over to get in touch with him. The code was for the agent to open the conversation with: "I am told the sea is frozen over at Mumbles Head", and Jones was to reply: "I am told the lighthouse is out of action". The agent went to the street where the master spy lived and knocked on the number he had been given. When the door was answered, the Russian began: "I am told the sea is frozen over at Mumbles Head", and the man replied: "I am Jones the baker. You want Jones the spy. He lives next door."

Mr. R. McNeil, President of Institute of Chartered Accountants, 1965:

Two Scots were climbing the Alps when one had a slight accident and was unable to get down to the hotel under his own steam. He and his friend took shelter in a hut and were snowed up for three days. Then an Alpine rescue team arrived. They heard the team approaching and called out: "Who's there?" Back came the answer, "The Red Cross". "No thank you", called out the Scotsmen. "We have already given".

TALE
ENDS...

The longer the spoke the greater the tyre.

Most things that are enjoyable in life are either immoral, illegal or fattening. *Sir Miles Thomas*

Mother whale to baby whale: "Remember you can only be shot at when you are spouting". — *The Lord Chancellor, Lord Kilmuir at banquet by Lord Mayor of London to Her Majesty's Judges, Mansion House, July 11, 1956.*

It is said one of the difficulties of marriage is not that it ties a man to a woman but that it separates him from all others. — *Dr. Charles Hill, Post-Master General, London Chamber of Commerce dinner, September 4, 1956.*

A paper published a heading, "Half the Council are crooks". It was asked to retract it, so it published the heading, "Half the Council are Not Crooks". — *Miss Rose Heilbron, Q.C. at dinner of Lloyd Memorial Home (Printing trade), Connaught Rooms, December 3, 1959.*

A friend went to Picasso and said, "May I have a word in your eye?" — *Lord Mancroft, Minister-without-Portfolio, Auctioneers and Estate Agents, Dorchester Hotel, October 31, 1957.*

A negro was overheard praying: "Use me as you will, O Lord, but preferably in an advisory capacity". — *Mr. Young, Headmaster of Charterhouse, at dinner of Corporation of the Sons of the Clergy, Mansion House, April 10, 1957.*

Conversation between two strawberries: "If we hadn't been in the same bed earlier in the year we would not have been in the same jam now". — *Dr. W.R. Wooldridge, at dinner of Institute of Meat, Innholders Hall, E.C. May 19, 1958.*

One bottle of milk to another: "I feel very fresh today". The other bottle of milk: "How terribly disappointing, I'm sterilised". — *Dr. W.R. Wooldridge, dinner of Institute of Meat, Innholders Hall, E.C., May 19, 1958.*

A young lady complained about the Commandments. She said: "They never tell you what to do; they only put ideas into your head". — *Lord Birkett, Lloyd Memorial Home (Printing trade), Connaught Rooms, December 1, 1960.*

A judge was asked what was the maximum penalty for bigamy and replied, "Two mothers-in-law". — *Sir Elwyn Jones, Attorney General, 1965.*

An advertisement I saw in an electricity show-room read: "Don't kill your wife with house-work — use an electric washing machine". — *Mr. Anthony Wedgwood Benn, Postmaster General, 1965.*

An army officer, on manoeuvres, asked a computer, "Shall I advance or retire?", and the machine answered: "Yes". "Yes, what?" asked the officer, and the reply came: "Yes, sir". — *Lord Pearce, Treasurer of Lincoln's Inn, 1966.*

A schoolgirl was asked in an examination paper to describe a convent. She wrote: "A convent is a place where virgins are confined". The inspector marked the paper: "This is either a misconception or a clerical error". — *Sir Charles Wheeler, President of Royal Academy of Arts.*

An ambassador at the end of a very enjoyable cocktail party, finding his last partner a very delightful lady, asked her: "You look so tired; do let me drive you to my flat". She answered: "Dear ambassador, I feel so tired I really must walk". — *Mr. Edward Heath at Institute of Export dinner, Connaught Rooms, 1965.*

A small girl was allowed to stay up for a dinner party and was asked to say grace for everyone. She went dumb. Her mother told her: "Just say what you heard Daddy say before breakfast this morning", and the girl said: "Oh Lord, why did you ask those damn people to dinner tonight". — *Viscount Amory, 1967.*

A stock-broker went to see a psychiatrist who asked him a lot of questions, concluding with: "What about your love-life?" The stock-broker replied: "Do you mean ordinary or preference?" — *Col. F.R. Mayer, President of National Association of British Manufacturers, 1966.*

A missionary met a lion in the jungle and thinking it was about to spring, he went down on his knees and began to pray. Nothing happened and opening his eyes he was amazed to see the lion also praying beside him. He asked the lion, "Are you a Christian lion?" and received the answer: "Yes, and I am saying grace". — *Mr. Arthur Bottomley, Secretary of State for Commonwealth Relations, 1965.*

A letter containing a cheque for £100 arrived at the Treasury and the writer said: "I can't sleep at night. For hours I think about it and have it on my conscience that ten years ago I did not declare tax on goods imported and I enclose a cheque for £100. If I find I still can't sleep I'll send you a cheque for the balance." — *Mr. Arthur Bottomley, Secretary of State for Commonwealth Relations, 1965.*